First Ladies

Melania Trump

Jennifer Strand

Launch!
An Imprint of Abdo Zoom
abdopublishing.com

abdopublishing.com

Published by Abdo Zoom, a division of ABDO, PO Box 398166, Minneapolis, Minnesota 55439.
Copyright © 2019 by Abdo Consulting Group, Inc. International copyrights reserved in all countries.
No part of this book may be reproduced in any form without written permission from the publisher.
Launch!™ is a trademark and logo of Abdo Zoom.

Printed in the United States of America, North Mankato, Minnesota.

052018
092018

THIS BOOK CONTAINS
RECYCLED MATERIALS

Photo Credits: Alamy, AP Images, Getty Images, Shutterstock, whitehouse.gov, ©Regine Mahaux cover/CC-BY-3.0 US

Production Contributors: Kenny Abdo, Jennie Forsberg, Grace Hansen, John Hansen

Design Contributors: Dorothy Toth, Neil Klinepier

Library of Congress Control Number: 2017960619

Publisher's Cataloging-in-Publication Data

Names: Strand, Jennifer, author.

Title: Melania Trump / by Jennifer Strand.

Description: Minneapolis, Minnesota : Abdo Zoom, 2019. | Series: First ladies |
    Includes online resources and index.

Identifiers: ISBN 9781532122866 (lib.bdg.) | ISBN 9781532123849 (ebook) |
    ISBN 9781532124334 (Read-to-me ebook)

Subjects: LCSH: Trump, Melania 1970-, Biography--Juvenile literature. | Presidents' spouses--United
    States--Biography--Juvenile literature. | First ladies (United States)--Biography--Juvenile literature.

Classification: DDC 973.93309 [B]--dc23

Table of Contents

Melania Trump

Melania Trump is the First Lady of the United States. Her husband Donald Trump is the 45th US President. She is known for her work with charities and her anti-**cyberbullying** plan.

Early Life

Melanija Knavs was born on April 26, 1970 in Novo Mesto, Slovenia.

She began modeling at five years old. At 18, Melanija Knavs changed her name to Melania Knauss. She worked all around Europe.

In 1996, Melania moved to New York City to focus on **modeling**. She met Donald Trump in 1998.

They were married in 2005. A year later their son Barron was born.

Leader

In 2015, Donald Trump made his presidency **bid**. Melania traveled the US with him. As First Lady, she would focus on helping women and children.

First Lady

Melania became the First Lady in 2017. She speaks about being a female **immigrant**. She hopes for gender fairness. Melania also visits schools to promote reading.

INTERNATIONAL
WOMEN OF COURAGE

Melania is also focusing on **cyberbullying.** She believes in kindness and respect for

She met with companies like
Google and Facebook. They
spoke about online safety for kids.

Legacy

Melania is the second foreign-born First Lady in US history. Louisa Adams was the first. Adams was from London, UK.

Melania works with many charities. Like the American Red Cross and the Boys & Girls Club.

Melania Trump

Born: April 26, 1970

Birthplace: Novo Mesto, Slovenia

Husband: Donald Trump

Years Served: 2017-

Political Party: Republican

Known For: Trump is the First Lady of the United States. She works with charities and focuses on anti-cyberbullying campaigns.

Key  Dates

1970: Melanija Knavs is born on April 26.

2001: Becomes a permanent resident of the United States.

2005: Melania Knauss marries Donald Trump on January 22.

2006: Becomes a United States citizen.

2017: Melania Trump is the First Lady. Donald Trump is the 45th president.

Glossary

bid – an offer to be the candidate for a certain political party.

cyberbullying – the use of the internet to bully or threaten a person.

Europe – the continent between Asia and the Atlantic Ocean. England, France, and Italy are some of the countries in Europe.

immigrant – a person who enters another country to live.

model – a person who wears and shows off the clothing for a designer.

Online Resources

For more information on
Melania Trump, please visit
abdobooklinks.com

Learn even more with the
Abdo Zoom Biographies database.
Visit **abdozoom.com** today!

Index